ABRAHAM LINCOLN

By
Sam Wellman

YOUNG READER'S CHRISTIAN LIBRARY

Illustrations by
Ken Save

A BARBOUR BOOK

ISBN 1-55748-602-6

Published by   Barbour and Company, Inc.
                P.O. Box 719
                Uhrichsville, OH 44683

Printed in the United States of America.

94 95 96 97 98 5 4 3 2 1

ABRAHAM LINCOLN

"CAN I GO EXPLORE NOW, FATHER?"

CHAPTER 1

"Can I go explore now, father?" asked Abe.

Tom Lincoln stopped chopping wood with an ax and gave Abe a stern look. "If you finished your chores, you can go play. But don't go down near the creek!"

Abe glanced down at Knob Creek. White water boiled over and around the rocks. He looked up a slope toward cliffs that shot straight up to the sky. The cliffs were dotted with stout cedar trees. Abe trudged up the slope.

Today another boy explored the slope above the log cabin where Abe lived. The boy wore yellow pants made from deer hide like Abe's father wore. Deer hide was called buckskin. The boy in buckskin put his fists on his hips and growled, "I'm Austin. What's your name, shirttail boy?"

"I'm Abe." All his life Abe had never worn pants at all. He wore a long itchy shirt that came to his knees. He never thought the shirt was unusual until now.

Austin squinted. "How come I've never seen you before? How old are you?"

"Thanks for asking." Abe loved to tell stories and this was one of his favorites. "I was born one morning over on Rock Spring farm. My sister Sarah woke up and saw father standing by the bed. Mother was in a heap of bear skins on the bed. She was holding a wrinkly red baby in a blanket. Sarah said my eyes and fists were closed tighter than walnuts. Black hair already plastered my head. Mother said 'let's name this boy Abraham after your father, Tom'...."

"How old are you?" asked Austin impatiently.

"I was born to Nancy and Tom Lincoln on the

"I'M ABE"

Lord's Day February 12 in the year 1809...."

"This is 1814. You're only five? You're as big as me and I'm seven. Can you wrestle, shirttail boy?" Austin's hands became spidery, ready to grab Abe.

"Like this?" Abe wrestled Austin to the ground. He let Austin get up right away. He knew when he wrestled Sarah if he held her down very long she got real mad.

Austin grinned. "Yes. Like that. When are you coming to school, Abe?"

"What do you do at school?"

"I learn reading and writing and ciphering. Ciphering is adding up and subtracting numbers."

Abe shrugged. "I know all 26 letters of the alphabet. I can count to a hundred. I can't go to school anyway. I have chores to do. I carry water. I fill the wood box. I hoe weeds. I slop the hogs. I poke seeds of corn into plowed ground. I fetch tools

ABE WRESTLED AUSTIN TO THE GROUND

for father...."

Austin interrupted him, "I get the idea: You're not coming to school."

And the boys played hide and seek in a field of corn.

A few days after Abe met Austin, Tom Lincoln hitched two horses to their big wagon. Tom lifted Abe into the wagon. Abe asked suspiciously, "Are you taking me to school?"

"No. We're going to Elizabethtown."

In Elizabethtown Abe saw a man with black skin being worked like a mule. The man wore a collar around his neck. The man's eyes never left the ground. Tom explained the black man was a "slave" owned by the mill owner.

Abe noticed something. His father's voice was cheerful and light when he had been telling funny stories in front of the general store. Now his voice

...A MAN WITH BLACK SKIN BEING WORKED LIKE A MULE

was sad and heavy—like the time they found their hog chewed up by a bear.

Abe asked, "How can a man own another man?"

Tom grunted, "It's the law here in Kentucky. All black folks in Kentucky are slaves."

Abe looked up and down the street. He saw lots of black folks—black women and children too. "What's law?"

"Rules white men make up."

"What's Kentucky?"

Tom had to laugh. "Elizabethtown here and the farm where we live are inside the state called Kentucky. There are seventeen other states in the United States. That's the nation we live in. Israel in the 'good book' is a nation."

All the way home Abe thought about law and states and nations and slaves. Things were simple on their farm. Abe knew how to make soap and candles.

ABE THOUGHT ABOUT LAW AND STATES AND NATIONS AND SLAVES

ABRAHAM LINCOLN

He saw how his mother ground corn into cornmeal, then baked it to make bread. He saw how his father, Tom, took rough walnut logs and made them into a smooth corner cabinet. But away from the farm Abe knew almost nothing. How would he ever know these things?

Every Sunday the Lincoln's walked to Little Mount Church. Preacher Elkins talked from the "good book" about the good news that Jesus had died and come alive again. But then the preacher closed the "good book" and frowned as he talked about how bad folks were who owned slaves.

When Abe or Sarah made them late to church Abe could hear Preacher Elkins preaching even though they were still a long way off. Preacher Elkins could talk softly too. And Abe watched how the preacher used his arms. Once in a while the preacher would throw his arms high, raise right up on his toes, and

THE PREACHER TALKED ABOUT BAD FOLKS WHO OWNED SLAVES

boom his voice off the ceiling.

On the way home Tom would say, "Mighty powerful preaching today..."

Mother would add, "No one can preach like Preacher Elkins."

One morning after a breakfast of eggs and bacon, Abe's mother said, "Abe has been shirttail boy long enough."

Tom didn't go outside to do chores like he usually did after breakfast. He grinned and said, "This I have to see."

"Here, Abe." Mother held up a pair of pants!

Abe fell down twice trying to get them on. Finally, he sat on a bench and tugged them on. The pants were made from yellow buckskin like Austin's. But Abe's pants were new and spotless. When he walked around in them they felt stiff and very heavy. He felt like he was wading through water.

MOTHER HELD UP A PAIR OF PANTS!

Mother said, "Put on your moccasins, Abe."

"Why? It didn't snow." Then he noticed Sarah was wearing a new dress. It was made of a kind of cotton cloth mother called calico. Abe muttered, "What's going on?"

Tom said, "Let's get going. It's two miles away. I'll give you a ride the first day."

Abe asked, "What's two miles away?"

Sarah laughed. "School, fancy pants."

"It's a blab school," said mother.

Abe rode in the wagon with Tom and Sarah to the rough cabin that was a school. Inside, Abe saw Austin jabbering out of a book. All twenty boys and girls sat on benches and jabbered lessons out loud at the same time so that the teacher would know they were working.

Abe blurted, "So that's why mother calls it a 'blab' school."

"WHAT'S GOING ON?"

Abe already knew the alphabet. It wasn't long before he blabbed words from a thin book called a "Speller." After one month he blabbed from the Speller a whole sentence of one syllable words, "Trust in the Lord with all your heart."

His teacher said, "That's a proverb, right out of the Bible."

"My mother reads that same proverb out of the 'good book' we have at home."

That fact hit Abe like a bolt of lightning! At home that night he began to read the "good book." On the very first page it said the "good book" was God's greatest gift!

Every night the Lincoln's sat together in front of the fireplace. While his mother read from the Bible Abe studied her. She was thin and very tall. Dark brown hair was parted in the middle. Her face looked wrinkled and hollow. She was missing some

HE BEGAN TO READ THE "GOOD BOOK"

teeth. She had a high forehead and yellow brown eyes. Long ago, when she was still called Nancy Hanks, his mother must have looked like Sarah.

And while his father told stories of every kind, Abe sized him up. Tom wasn't much taller than mother. But his shoulders were wide, his arms thick. Abe wasn't like him that way. Abe was thin and gawky. When Abe peered at himself in a mud puddle, the only things that looked like they belonged on his father were his coarse black hair and deep-set gray eyes.

There were silent times by the fire, too. Mother sewed. Tom cleaned his carpenter tools. Abe and Sarah did spelling and grammar lessons from their Speller. The Speller used examples from the Bible. For Abe and Sarah the "good book" was everywhere. God's Word was as basic to their life as air. They never ate a meal before Tom said, "Fit and

THERE WERE SILENT TIMES BY THE FIRE

prepare us for humble service for Christ's sake. Amen."

Abe practiced writing, too. Paper was far too precious to use. If he was in front of the fire, he blackened words on firewood with a piece of charcoal. If he was outside the cabin, he fingered words in the dirt or mud or snow.

But sometimes he just had fun exploring with Austin.

One time Abe's father had been gone on a trip nearly a month. Wintry clouds had been scraping the cliff tops and raining hard for a week. One morning the sun shone again. So Abe explored along the banks of Knob Creek with Austin. The water in Knob Creek didn't boil around the rocks like it usually did. No rocks could be seen at all.

Abe said, "The water looks calm."

"The water only looks calm because it's so deep

"THE WATER LOOKS CALM"

and muddy. It's swifter than it's ever been." Austin sounded scared. "Look. It cut into the bank and knocked that old birch tree over."

"The tree toppled right across Knob Creek!" yelled Abe. "It's a bridge!" He jumped up on the dark scaly bark. "We can see what's over on the other side."

Austin cried, "You better not! You can't swim!"

Abe slipped. The last thing he saw before he thrashed into the creek was Austin's mouth drop open in horror.

ABE SLIPPED!

"OH PLEASE SAVE ME, JESUS..."

CHAPTER 2

Icy water yanked Abe along like a hundred horses. He clawed weeds at the bank's edge as he was swept by.

He saw Austin running along the bank beside him. The creek rolled Abe over. Water rushed into his nose. Pain stung below his eyes and inside his forehead. He tried to scream. Water choked him. He kicked a rock with his toe. He was sinking. He prayed, "Oh please save me, Jesus...."

Abe beat his arms against the crushing water. His fingers touched something. He grabbed.

He held something! If only he could pull himself to the bank. But he was too weak. He would never make it. He couldn't breathe. Everything was spinning, going black.

Something whacked him on the back. He gagged.

The creek gushed from his throat. Again and again he gagged. His back hurt. His stomach ached. His throat burned.

"Wake up, Abe!" It was Austin's voice.

Abe opened his eyes. He was on the bank. A branch was by his face. He sputtered, "I...I...I'm alive."

Austin said, "It's a good thing you grabbed that branch so I could haul you in."

Abe shivered from more than cold. It was quite a while before he said, "I came one branch from dying."

"It was more than a branch," said Austin. "It was like your mother always says: God has a plan for you, Abe."

Abe was silent. He wasn't sure Austin was right. Could a boy be so foolish he could actually defeat God's plan? It was something very important to

"I...I...I'M ALIVE!"

think about.

Three weeks before Christmas, father Tom returned from his trip. That first night back, while all four Lincoln's warmed in front of a fire roaring in the fireplace, Tom said, "We're going to move to a new state called Indiana."

Mother explained, "Father and I decided we have to leave Kentucky. Our neighbors are buying more and more slaves. In Indiana no man can be made a slave."

Abe knew Indiana must be some place special.

Into the big wagon they loaded everything they owned except their furniture. It was easier for Tom to make new furniture at their new home. Two horses pulled the wagon. Tied behind the wagon were two more horses and one cow. Three hounds chased each other around the wagon.

Abe was scared when he climbed up into the

"WE'RE MOVING TO A NEW STATE CALLED INDIANA"

wagon box. But he didn't complain. Tom turned on the wagon seat to say, "I'm sorry you children are cold. But winter is the best time to move. We're living off food we salted and dried anyway. And these roads are frozen solid as rock instead of being knee-deep in mud."

They clopped along the frozen mud road mile after mile. Chickens clucked in wooden cages and hogs grunted right next to Abe. He was sad as he remembered all the times he and Austin played together. Would he ever see Austin again?

The wagon stopped....

"I never saw such a thing!" shouted Sarah.

The gleaming ribbon of water was ten times wider than Abe could skip a flat rock. Tom laughed. "Only the men on the barges, flatboats, and bit steamboats know how many times deeper than Abe's nose that Ohio River is."

"I NEVER SAW SUCH A THING!"

Mother beamed, "On the other side is Indiana."

A ferry boat took them across the Ohio River and they headed the wagon into woods folks called "rough." Indiana had "rough" like Abe had never seen before. Oak, sycamore, hackberry, ash, poplar, maple, and beech trees towered into the sky. Grapevines as thick as small trees webbed all the trees and undergrowth together.

"A snake has to work hard to squeeze through this rough," joked Tom. But he had to hack and chop from dawn to dusk, day after day, to clear the way for the wagon.

Tom seemed to relax after they reached a high area. He said, "This land is just above Little Pigeon Creek."

"Look. A half-face." Abe pointed at a crude, three-sided lean-to called a half-faced camp. Three walls were made of logs and boughs. The fourth side

"ON THE OTHER SIDE IS INDIANA!"

was open. "Someone lives here," said Abe.

"I built that." Tom waved around them. "This is the land I claimed."

Abe jumped out of the wagon. "So this is where you were while you were gone."

Tom nodded. "I stacked brush on each corner to mark our claim. The corners mark a square one-half mile on each side. Our land is rich in oak and hickory trees. Natural salt licks attract all kinds of wild critters. Springs seep good water north of the half-face. Over yonder to the east, there's a small stream moseying right across our land."

The three hounds were already learning the new property. Abe heard them way off somewhere in the tangled rough, baying and yelping.

Tom smiled. "Within one year, I have to ride up to the town of Vincennes. I have to pay $80 to the government to get a paper that proves we own this

"SO THIS IS WHERE YOU WERE..."

160 acres." He frowned. "We'll still owe them $240."

Abe whistled. "This land costs two whole dollars per acre!"

· Mother said, "Let's get settled. Abe, unload a bag of cornmeal and a ham for supper. Sarah, spread leaves over the ground in the half-face."

Tom grabbed his ax. "I'll take care of the animals."

Tom build a shelter and corral for the horses and the cow. The sky was dark as he finished a separate one for the hogs. He saw Abe had moved the cages full of chickens into the half-face. A big fire had to be kept blazing there all the time in place of a fourth wall.

Tom said, "We'll build a chicken coop tomorrow. Then we'll start the cabin. We have two sharp axes."

Two axes! It was the first night Abe didn't fall

"WE'LL STILL OWE THEM 240 DOLLARS"

asleep thinking how much he missed Austin. Under wool blankets and bearskins, with hens clucking softly by his head, Abe dreamed of swinging the ax. Sometime in the night the hounds returned, panting and exhausted.

The next morning Tom said, "Let's get started." He handed seven-year-old Abe an ax.

Tom chopped down trees one foot thick that could be cut into logs twenty feet long. They needed thirty-two of these logs, eight for each wall. Abe whacked off the limbs. He notched the ends, so the logs would lock together.

They cut shorter logs for the gables, the uppermost triangle-shaped parts of the walls at each end of the cabin. They made a nice sloping roof by overlapping wood shingles on thin logs that stretched from gable to gable. Inside the cabin, Tom placed beams from wall to wall eight feet above the floor. He pounded

"LET'S GET STARTED"

stout wood pegs up one wall.

Abe asked, "Why do you need those pegs?"

"You and Sarah will need them."

Abe shrugged. "What for?"

Tom laughed. "To climb up to the loft I'm going to build on the beams. That's where you and Sarah will sleep."

Abe and Sarah "chinked" thin slabs of wood in the cracks between the logs. After chinking, they daubed mud between the logs. To Abe the cabin was wonderful. His family made it right out of the forest. It was solid and safe and smelled of fresh cut wood.

Abe bragged, "We made the cabin in just four days."

"With God's mercy," said mother.

"You handle an ax like a man, Abe." Tom looked puzzled, just like the time mother convinced him Abe was really reading the Bible and not reciting it

ABRAHAM LINCOLN

TO ABE THE CABIN WAS WONDERFUL

from memory.

Sarah scanned the thick rough woods around the cabin. "When are we going back to school?"

Tom said, "Folks can't get a teacher to come here yet. You can school yourself."

Abe practiced reading and writing every evening. A neighbor told Tom he wanted to write his mother in Kentucky but didn't know how to write. Tom told him maybe Abe could write a letter for him. So Abe not only wrote the letter but worked out the very best way to write what the neighbor wanted to say. Soon other neighbors asked Abe to write letters for them. Tom heard folks at Gentry's store talking about how Abe was ahead of other boys his age. He was taller. He could write. And how he could swing an ax!

Before the next winter, Abe's aunt and uncle, the Sparrows, and their son, Dennis Hanks, moved from Kentucky to live near the Lincoln's. Although

"YOU CAN SCHOOL YOURSELF"

ABRAHAM LINCOLN

Dennis was several years older than Abraham, the two cousins became friends. When they found time, seventeen-year-old Dennis and Abe talked as equals: Dennis, an older fun-loving joker, and Abe, a younger "wizard" folks talked about.

Tom Lincoln got a copy of *Aesop's Fables*. Abe read it through and through. The fables weren't as deep and moving as the parables Jesus told in the Bible, but a fable like the fox and the grapes was fun to read. Abe loved how fables and parables helped him understand life better. He turned stories inside and out, up and down, front and back. None of the Lincolns got much sleep any night Abe kept talking about what a fable or a parable meant.

"Jumping Jehoshaphat," exclaimed Tom. "I never saw anyone chew on an idea like you, Abe. You're like a Indian woman chewing deer hide until it's soft. You won't let go of it until you've got it exactly the

ABE KEPT TALKING ABOUT WHAT A PARABLE MEANT

way it's supposed to be."

Mother added, "The only time Abe loses his temper is when he doesn't understand something he reads or hears."

Once in while now, Abe got to ride a horse alone to the mill. He took a bag of corn to grind into flour. The mill was the kind where the customer had to use his own horse to grind the corn. Abe hitched his horse to the beam and began strolling behind the horse on its endless circular path. It seemed like it would take forever.

"Get up, you old horse!" he yelled without thinking.

The frightened horse whinnied.

As quickly as a flick of the horse's tail everything went black for Abe.

EVERYTHING WENT BLACK FOR ABE

"I CAN'T GET A PULSE"

CHAPTER 3

Abe drifted through space too black and too deep to ever put in words.

He heard a man cry, "I can't get a pulse. The poor boy is dead."

Abe opened his eyes. He was looking at the sky. Where was the horse? He felt the pebbly ground sticking in his back.

A whiskery face looked down at him "Abe's alive!" The face belonged to the owner of the mill.

Abe asked, "What happened, Mr. Gordon?"

Mr. Gordon pressed a wet rag against Abe's forehead. "You just lay down for a spell. Your horse almost plumb kicked your head off, Abe." He whispered to someone. "I was sure Abe was dead."

After a while Abe got up. A huge lump on his forehead throbbed pain with every heartbeat. As he rode the horse home, he recited verses memorized from the Bible. His mind worked all right. He didn't like to think about what had happened. That was the second time he almost died.

Tom Lincoln got Abe and Sarah a copy of *Pilgrim's Progress*. Abe read *Pilgrim's Progress* again and again just like other books. It told of a pilgrim's journey to save his soul from hell. The pilgrim survived one disaster after another and succeeded despite constant danger. Abe's own life on the frontier didn't always seem dangerous. That made it even more dangerous. One careless moment could end his life. He remembered the horse at the mill.

At the front of the book was a sketch of the life of the Englishman who wrote the book. Abe read that John Bunyan was "raised from the deepest obscurity...to be uncommonly useful for mankind." Every time Abe read that passage his heart was

HE RECITED VERSES MEMORIZED FROM THE BIBLE

pounding so hard he had to stop.

He prayed, "How could anyone be more obscure than I am out here in the woods? Maybe I too can be uncommonly useful. Is that your plan for me, God?" Yet he knew how Bunyan's pilgrim suffered one disaster after another. Was that God's plan for Abe? Things were very pleasant right now on their farm. Every night he talked with his family and read in front of the fire. And he heard folks found a teacher. Abe might even get some schooling once in a while.

Abe loved his job in the forest. Someday corn would stretch far beyond their cabin. Abe's job was to chop out bushes and grapevines growing under the trees. Tom was always within shouting distance. But Abe felt like he worked alone. He knew other folks were working just like him all around the forest. He imagined how they all cleared land farther and farther away from their cabins. Would the day

ABE LOVED HIS JOB IN THE FOREST

ever come when they would all break out of the forest suddenly and he would see neighbors standing everywhere?

Abe never felt alone. The forest chattered and squeaked and bellowed with critters. It was a rare day a flock of passenger pigeons didn't darken the sky. Squirrels scolded him from the trees. Skunks ambled by fearlessly, armed with stinging smell. Wildcats hissed but were never seen. Blue-skinned lizards darted away. Snakes slithered under leaves. Wasps buzzed him from papery nests.

Raccoons burst like fat fur balls from undergrowth to scurry up a tree. All day long Abe saw possums, groundhogs, badgers, mink, deer, foxes, toads, turkeys, ducks, and a hundred kinds of insects he couldn't name. The critters rustled, chattered, cheeped, and grunted all around him.

"Jumping Jehoshaphat," he mimicked his father.

"JUMPING JEHOSHAPHAT"

"How you critters can carry on."

The second summer in Indiana was not like the first summer. Tom grumbled, "It's too hot. It's too dry. I don't like this. Hot dry summers are not good."

Abe said, "It's not so bad if you go swimming now and again." Abe heard about the local swimming hole on Little Pigeon Creek from Dennis Hanks. Abe was always hinting that he should be allowed to go there too.

Abe's mother and father exchanged worried looks. Abe thought they worried about him swimming.

One late summer evening Tom was too quiet by the fire. His face so darkened by the sun looked white. Finally he said, "I think our old cow has got the trembles."

"Trembles!" Mother, who was always calm, had to calm herself before she asked, "Are you sure she isn't just old?"

Tom replied softly, "We'll wait and see. Nobody

"I THINK OUR OLD COW HAS GOT THE TREMBLES"

drink any milk or eat any cheese. Go to bed, children."

And Tom left the cabin for a while.

Abe and Sarah climbed into the loft. Abe asked Sarah when did she last drink milk? She couldn't remember. And he asked her when did she last eat cheese? She wasn't sure when. Abe's mouth felt thick and cottony. He didn't like the taste of milk. He wasn't much of an eater at all. But he tried to remember: When did he last drink milk? When did he last eat cheese?

Laying up in the loft that night, Abe heard his father come back. Tom told Mother he had warned neighbors. Tom said in a worried whisper that because of the dry summer the old cow had grazed far back into the woods. Two days later the cow died.

Tom sat the children down. "It's certain now. Our old cow had the milk fever. Cows get it in hot dry summers. The disease doesn't stop at the cow.

WHEN DID HE LAST DRINK MILK?

Somehow it poisons the cow's milk. Somehow it poisons some folks who drink the cow's milk or eat cheese made from the cow's milk."

Dennis Hanks pounded the door next morning. He sobbed. "Mr. Sparrow woke up with a white tongue!"

Abe never heard such fear in Dennis before.

Mother gasped, "A white coating on the tongue is the first sure sign of milk fever!" And she rushed to help Mrs. Sparrow nurse Mr. Sparrow. When she came back that evening she said grimly, "His stomach is burning—the second sure sign. He made out a will!"

Tom said, "Let us pray there is no third sign: a brown tongue."

The next day Mrs. Sparrow got a white tongue! Mr. Sparrow's tongue did turn brown and he died. In a daze, Mrs. Sparrow realized she would likely follow her husband. Abe's mother nursed her.

"MR. SPARROW WOKE UP WITH A WHITE TONGUE!"

Sarah helped.

Abe helped his father saw planks of black cherry wood. Then Tom planed them smooth. Abe whittled pegs. The pegs would hold on the lid of the coffin. Mr. Sparrow's coffin was as fine as Tom could make it in such a short time. Tom didn't say anything, but Abe knew he started a second coffin for Mrs. Sparrow. And there were graves to dig deep into the yellow Indiana soil.

One morning when Nancy came back to the cabin Tom asked her, "How is Mrs. Sparrow?"

Nancy winced as she sat down. "She's still alive, but not for long. She'll be gone by afternoon or evening."

Tom said, "Rest a while before you go back."

Abe couldn't remember seeing his mother so tired. She had been tired a lot since coming to Indiana, but today she looked old, too. She seemed far older than thirty-four.

"SHE'LL BE GONE BY AFTERNOON OR EVENING"

Mother said, "I won't be going back, Tom."

Fear erupted inside Abe as if he had just heard a thousand rattlesnakes all around him.

He cried, "Mother has milk fever!"

Abe's life seemed to come to a stop. Mother was lying in bed, her face chalk white. He prayed and prayed for her life to be spared. But she got the second sign, then the third. Life no longer made any sense to Abe.

Mother was calm. She smiled at Abe and Sarah. "We will be parting soon. This is a very sad time. But we can not always understand our heavenly Father's ways. You children won't think so, but I'm lucky. It won't be long until I see our Savior, Jesus."

Abe was nine years old when Nancy Lincoln died. He and Sarah brooded for their mother. And what if their father got milk fever?

Days after Mother was buried on a knoll in sight of the cabin, Tom took Abe and Sarah by the hand and

ABE WAS NINE YEARS OLD WHEN NANCY LINCOLN DIED

marched them down the familiar trail to Jim Gentry's store. Then he turned and walked them down a strange trail. It took them one hour to reach a flat-roofed cabin.

Tom said, "You children must go on with your life."

Abe heard a chorus of voices. Tom opened the door and nudged Abe and Sarah inside. Heads of children turned to gawk at them. The room fell into silence.

Tom handed a man something wrapped in cloth. Tom said, "These children are Sarah and Abe Lincoln."

And the man said, "Howdy do! I'm Andrew Crawford. Thanks kindly for the bacon. Sit down, Sarah and Abe. Take off that coonskin cap, Abe."

Tom Lincoln turned and left.

Andrew Crawford taught a "blab" school. But he spent the whole morning on manners. Pupils

"HOWDY DO! I'M ANDREW CRAWFORD"

practiced saying a cheerful "howdy do!" When a boy entered a room he took off his cap. Outside, boys tipped their caps and introduced themselves. Girls curtsied. Boys and girls both practiced opening doors for older folks.

Abe ate his lunch of corn dodgers and dried apples next to a boy who was older but about Abe's size.

The boy said, "Howdy do, Abe. I'm Matt Gentry."

"Your father must run the general store."

"Yes, he does. Isn't your father the carpenter?"

Abe was stunned. He thought of his father, Tom, as a farmer. Matt called his father a carpenter, a man who made things out of wood. That made Abe the "carpenter's son." He had read those very words in the "good book" a hundred times. It took his breath away.

"ISN'T YOUR FATHER THE CARPENTER?"

WOULD THEY SPEND CHRISTMAS ALONE?

CHAPTER 4

Of course Abe knew the "carpenter's son" Jesus was really the son of God. Abe was only a boy. Still he wanted to believe it was a sign from God that he might amount to something.

The next year was rough on twelve-year-old Sarah. She worked hard to do all the work her mother had done in the cabin and garden. Abe and Tom helped but weren't as particular as Sarah. And besides, they had work in the fields and forests to do.

One month before Christmas, Tom said, "Children, I have to go on a trip." And Tom rode off on a horse without another word of explanation.

Abe was only ten. He had never felt more hopeless. He acted cheerful for Sarah. Every night he prayed for his father to return.

Would they spend Christmas alone?

What if his father never came back at all?

A few days before Christmas, Abe and Sarah were inside the cabin when they heard a wagon rattling up the trail.

"Maybe it's father," yelled Sarah.

"He didn't take a wagon," reasoned Abe glumly, but he ran out of the cabin with Sarah. He couldn't give up hope.

Off the wagon jumped a boy about half as tall as Abe. He stuck out his chest. "I'm John. I'm seven."

A girl stepped down. "I'm Elizabeth. I'm nine." She pointed at a young girl clinging to the wagon. "That's Matilda. She's five."

Abe blurted, "Are you folks just passing through?"

Suddenly Tom stood there with a woman. He said, "This is Sally, your new mother. All the way from Elizabethtown."

Abe was flabbergasted. What could he say?

"THIS IS SALLY, YOUR NEW MOTHER"

Before he could think of anything to say, Sally hugged him. And Abe looked into one of the kindest faces he had ever seen. She handed Abe two books he had never read before: *Robinson Crusoe* and *Arabian Knights*. So this was how God answered his prayers. Sally was a thousand times better than anything he asked for.

Now Abe remembered his mother saying how kind the widow Sally Johnston was. Tom had certainly remembered.

Sally didn't come empty-handed. Abe helped Tom unload a chest of drawers, a table, some chairs, a box of clothing, a box of bedding, and many kitchen utensils. Tom built the second bedstead for the three girls. Abe and John would sleep in the loft.

The new family celebrated the birth of Jesus. Sally roasted a turkey Tom shot, stuffed with roots and nuts the children had gathered in the forest.

...ONE OF THE KINDEST FACES HE EVER SAW

When Sally saw the bounty from Sarah's labor in the garden she gave her a special hug. She cried, "Sarah has put up peas, turnips, beets, radishes, onions, and look at all the potatoes. What treasures!"

That was when Abe realized Sally and her children must have had a rough time, too. All the food he took for granted was treasure to them. In the Dutch oven in the fireplace, Sally baked johnnycakes made from cornmeal, water, and butter. They had syrup from sugar maples. They ate on pewter dishes. Abe felt like he was being born into something special again.

Abe wouldn't rest until something was done he promised his real mother as she was dying. He had written Preacher Elkins in Kentucky. And when the preacher finally came to Indiana to visit a son, he went with the Lincolns to Nancy's grave. Abe was sure his mother heard preacher Elkins' eulogy. After

HE WENT WITH THE LINCOLN'S TO NANCY'S GRAVE

that Abe didn't feel guilty for being so happy with his new mother. He was sure it was God's plan.

In the forest, Abe was handling an ax like a man. His long arms delivered such a powerful stroke he buried the ax deeper into the wood than most men. One neighbor, hearing how fast the trees fell, thought there were several men working back in the rough. No, said Tom, it was only Abe. And now John helped Abe by stacking brush against trees.

Abe told story after story to John.

And John had stories to tell. He didn't have the kind of stories Abe craved, like the story that there was a new state west of Indiana called Illinois. But John had seen some mighty strange characters come and go in Elizabethtown. After all, he had lived only one block from Hardin County courthouse. His favorite story was about the circus that came to town. Each time he told it the elephant got bigger and the

ONE NEIGHBOR THOUGHT THERE WERE SEVERAL MEN WORKING

lion roared louder and the trained seal got smarter.

Abe put down his ax and sighed. "Of course, John, you know we have real bears, wolves, and panthers prowling loose right here in this forest."

John's voice was dry. "I do hear thrashing around our cabin at night." He laughed nervously. "I bet it's just the hounds."

Abe was serious. "A panther jumped the Bowers boy and girl a few years ago."

John gulped. "A panther?"

Abe said, "A panther is a hermit of an animal. It doesn't hang around roads and trails during the day." He gave John a stern look. "Just don't take any shortcuts through the forest."

"I'll remember that." John frowned, probably wondering if Abe was trying to scare him.

Abe should have let the forest speak for itself.

A huge black form appeared from out of nowhere.

"I'LL REMEMBER THAT"

It seemed taller than the trees. The bear sniffed the air, smelled the sweat of boys, and thundered back into the brush.

By 1821 when Abe was twelve, the Lincolns and their neighbors had been clearing land and planting corn for five years. The area opened up just as Abe had imagined it years earlier. Once, Abe felt the Lincolns were isolated. Now, within one mile of the Lincoln cabin were seven other cabins. Abe sat down one day and scratched a mark in the yellow soil for every child in those seven cabins.

He whistled. "Forty young folks! And that doesn't include the five of us."

Church had been held for many years, but never in a special building. It was time to build a regular church building. And who was better qualified to supervise the construction than the best carpenter in the county: Tom Lincoln? So he and neighbors built

"FORTY YOUNG FOLKS!"

a solid church 26 feet by 30 feet. Tom and Sally were official members.

The children went to the church every Sunday, too. But in those days it was not the custom to make them official members. Men and women became members when they got married like Elizabeth did that same year when she married Dennis Hanks. She and Dennis lived in a cabin one mile east of the Lincolns.

Abe became a sexton in the church. He ordered supplies and kept records. As he swept the floor he would remember the persuasion in Preacher Elkins' voice and his gestures. Every Sunday morning he listened to a sermon, too. He got in the habit of preaching a sermon himself Sunday afternoon.

If Abe was still preaching to John and Matilda on Monday, Tom would notice no one was working and say, "Abe must be on the stump again." And Tom would remind Abe and his audience the heavenly

HE GOT IN THE HABIT OF PREACHING A SERMON HIMSELF

Father wished them to earn their daily bread.

Abe got the habit of taking a book with him everywhere. It was as natural as grabbing an apple. Every moment he took a break from work he read. He treasured one new book written by Ben Franklin about himself. Franklin detailed how he improved himself by setting goals for each day and at the end of the day reviewed how well he succeeded. Abe understood Franklin's ambition perfectly. Abe had a burning desire to improve himself. He loved the woods, but he didn't want to spend a lifetime cutting down trees. And he knew farming was not for him as important as it was to raise food for folks to eat.

A second book thrilled him even more. It told the life of George Washington. Abe had never known of such a sense of duty—other than the saints in the Bible. Here was a man who lived only a few years before Abe was born. He was a man of action, but

ABE HAD A BURNING DESIRE TO IMPROVE HIMSELF

he showed such moral perfection that Abe was astounded. Washington would forever be Abe's ideal American. Abe couldn't hear the word "patriot" without thinking of George Washington. And the fact that Washington believed it was his duty to carry out God's plan confirmed his perfection for Abe.

In the yellow soil Abe scratched the words: "Good boys who to their books apply/Will all be great to me by and by." Abe began to think how governments worked. He began to see why man-made laws were necessary in addition to God's commandments in the Bible. The Bible didn't say exactly how folks paid for a school. It didn't say how folks should determine whether a man accused of a crime was innocent or guilty. Abe knew man-made laws fell short of being perfect. Otherwise, white folks wouldn't own black slaves. How did that happen? He burned to

ASHINGTON WOULD FOREVER BE ABE'S IDEAL AMERICAN

know. Tom told him a man named Henry Clay from Kentucky persuaded folks to accept the "Missouri Compromise." That meant the new state of Missouri would permit slaves, but no new states north of a certain line would allow slaves. When Abe talked to John about it, John just shook his head. Why talk about such complicated things? John just wanted to talk about the elephants.

Years passed. Sarah got married. Now she was a neighbor. Abe visited courtrooms whenever he could. Folks were puzzled by the gangly young giant. What would become of him? He was a sexton in the church. He could split rails faster than anyone else. He could wrestle anyone to the ground. He talked about things nobody but a lawyer or a teacher could understand. But he didn't seem cut out for doing anything in particular.

And then, once again, tragedy struck.

YEARS PASSED

ABE COULDN'T FRITTER HIS LIFE AWAY

CHAPTER 5

Sadness overwhelmed Abe again. Sarah, the sweet girl who had been sister, brother, and mother to Abe, died giving birth to a baby. Abe wanted to lash out at something with his sinewy, ax-wielding arms—but he could do nothing but pray Sarah was with Jesus in heaven.

Friend Matt Gentry lost his mind. One moment Matt was fine. The next moment he was babbling, lost somewhere beyond reach. Abe waited for Matt to get better. But he didn't get better. It seemed to Abe as if by not being able to decide what to do in life, he was waiting around until something bad happened to him too. Abe couldn't fritter his life away. Tom urged him to try other things.

Abe tried ferrying folks across the Ohio River. Allen Gentry offered Abe a different job. Allen was going to pilot a flatboat of corn and pork all the way to New Orleans. Abe accepted the offer. Tom had taken a flatboat to New Orleans himself—one year before Sarah was born. Maybe Abe would get married when he got back. He could hardly imagine any girl who would be interested in such a strange young man as himself.

The flatboat drifted downriver into ever warmer, wetter air. While tied to shore one night near Baton Rouge, the flatboat was attacked by thieves. Abe and Allen could have jumped in the river and saved themselves, but they refused to surrender their cargo. The thieves were shocked to see a towering fury leaping about in the moonlight—a fury who broke bones with a thunderous whacking ax handle. The attackers fled, thankful to be alive. And Abe thanked God to be alive.

The trip to New Orleans became a bad dream to

A TOWERING FURY LEAPING ABOUT IN THE MOONLIGHT

Abe. He saw slaves auctioned. He saw white men poke fingers into black people as if they were livestock. New Orleans seemed thousands of years old, with sin everywhere. He couldn't wait to get home again. But what would he do with his life when he got back home? He would turn twenty years old on the way back to Indiana on a steamboat. All the way on the Mississippi River to Cairo, Abe prayed. All the way up the Ohio River to Troy in Indiana, he prayed. And he noticed the boat seemed to go in every direction on the looping rivers yet stayed on a relentless course from New Orleans to Troy.

The Gentrys liked Abe. He worked in their store after he got back. It would have been hard to find a better clerk than Abe. He was a true pioneer. So he knew what folks needed. And he was so strong he could lift a keg full of nails into a wagon. He could read. He knew how to work with numbers. He could

ABE KNEW WHAT FOLKS NEEDED

keep records. He was honest.

And more than one newcomer was startled enough to blurt, "A giant!" Abe now towered six feet four inches tall and weighed over two hundred lean-muscled pounds.

Working in the store was to Abe's liking, too. It seemed like folks hadn't stopped talking politics since the national election the year before. Andrew Jackson, the great hero of the War of 1812, ran against President John Quincy Adams. Jackson, calling himself a Democrat, won the election. Abe loved to hear folks talk politics.

Abe felt he could prosper as a clerk, too. Had God answered his prayers? He still lived with his father but that wasn't unusual for a man his age. The law even said he had to give his earnings to his father until he turned twenty-one. Not that Tom needed Abe's money. Tom Lincoln had prospered from his

ABE LOVED TO HEAR FOLKS TALK POLITICS

dozen years in Indiana. He owned one hundred hogs. He harvested many acres of corn. He started building a house for Sally that no one would call a cabin.

And then Sally's son-in-law did something that turned the Lincolns' world upside down.

Squire Hall, the husband of Matilda, and Dennis Hanks, the husband of Elizabeth, announced they were moving west—to the state of Illinois. Sally couldn't bear being separated from her daughters. Abe suddenly discovered Tom and Sally were going to Illinois, too!

Abe went along. Of course, they moved in the winter. They traveled in two wagons. The trip was two hundred miles over frozen mud and ice-covered streams. But the long cold journey in wagons gave Abe time to think. He was grown now. It was time for him to fly from the nest. As always, he prayed that

IT WAS TIME FOR HIM TO FLY FROM THE NEST

God would let him do what was right. The three families stopped in central Illinois, just west of Decatur. Once again, Tom and Abe built a cabin plus corrals and a shed for the livestock.

Abe was not happy that year of 1830. He felt more out of place than ever. He didn't even have his clerking job now. He didn't want to spend his life always clearing new land, always plowing new soil. Winter came again. And it was the kind of winter that ices the land only once in a hundred years. After a blizzard dumped deep snow, the temperature never got above zero for two months!

"Who can withstand God's icy blast?" said Abe to Tom and Sally. The verse from Psalm 147 never seemed more true.

The winter was very hard on the newcomers because they didn't have large stores of food. But they survived. And by the time of spring thaws,

"WHO CAN WITHSTAND GOD'S ICY BLAST?"

everyone was anxious to get outside and work. Abe was so desperate to get some business, he was talked into piloting a flatboat of some goods to New Orleans again. On the way down to the Sangamon River the flatboat ran aground for a while at a village called New Salem. Months later, after Abe sold the corn and pork at New Orleans, he returned to Tom and Sally to say farewell. Then Abe headed for the village of New Salem. He was twenty-two and on his own at last.

He clerked in New Salem. He was so good at it, most folks quickly came to respect him. But New Salem was not like living on a farm. Rough men lived in villages. Jack Armstrong, the leader of the "Clary Grove gang," challenged the newcomer to wrestle. But Armstrong was no match for a giant who had labored in the farm and forest almost every waking hour of his life.

HE WAS TWENTY TWO AND ON HIS OWN AT LAST

Jack Armstrong was a good loser. Abe was nothing like the roughnecks Jack knew. Abe didn't drink alcohol. He didn't smoke tobacco. But Abe did know how to poke fun at himself. He did tell jokes. He did have a story for every situation. He never lied. And he was a wizard at figuring things out—practical things, too. Abe made a friend for life in Jack Armstrong.

New Salem was different from the farm in another way, too. Men met to debate each other. They called themselves "free-thinkers" and Abe quickly found they thought they were free to think and say anything. Abe was shocked. It was the first time he had ever heard men question out loud whether Jesus was God. They wondered if Adam really did sin—and, if he did sin, did Jesus really pay for that sin? They wondered why if God was good, He would allow death and pain in the world. They questioned everything.

THEY QUESTIONED EVERYTHING

It wasn't as if Abe hadn't asked these questions. He had. Before he could read, the true answers to his questions came from his mother's lips. And after he could read, he found the true answers himself in the Bible. Abe realized that, as much as he hated their attitude about Jesus, he had asked similar questions. So, if he denied these "free-thinkers" the right to speak out, he would be a hypocrite.

Maybe he could change some of their minds. He could not have done that to men who kept their doubts secret and pretended to believe in Jesus. Some of the men snickered at Abe. Did this backwoods roughneck who just whipped Jack Armstrong in the dusty street think he could debate educated men like a schoolmaster and a doctor?

But Abe knew the Bible by heart and he could remember verses to advance his arguments. He especially liked to make the point that the souls of all

HE COULD REMEMBER VERSES TO ADVANCE HIS ARGUMENTS

folks could be saved. No one was picked ahead of time to go to hell. He believed God had a plan for everyone, but folks still had to make their own choices to be saved.

He raised his arms toward the ceiling and quoted Saint Paul in I Corinthians 15:22: "For as in Adam all die, even so in Christ shall all be made alive...."

The "free-thinkers" argued with Abe. And Abe countered their arguments with reasoned arguments from the Bible. Their challenge was actually strengthening his spiritual armor. After a while, Abe could tell the men were amazed a roughneck like Abe had such power to reason and persuade. He worried about being too proud of himself. After all, he had God's Word to help him.

After one debate the doctor admitted, "You know, Abe, I really do believe Jesus is God."

Abe was surprised. "Why, you just argued hot and

" I REALLY DO BELIEVE JESUS IS GOD "

heavy in a debate that there is no God at all."

The doctor said, "I just like to take different sides in a debate. It helps me think things out better."

Abe replied, "I see debating is a powerful way of turning a subject inside and out." The truth was that Abe had always done that. He debated within himself.

The doctor said, "Abe, you're very good at speaking, but you still need more practice."

"Practice for what?" Abe sensed something very big was happening to him.

"PRACTICE FOR WHAT?"

"DO YOU WANT ME TO RUN FOR THE LEGISLATURE?"

CHAPTER 6

The doctor put his hand up on Abe's shoulder.

"Abe," he said. "Folks, educated and uneducated, want a righteous, God-fearing man to represent their needs in the state legislature—the group of men who make the laws of Illinois. The people decide which man that is going to be with their votes. So a man has to know how to speak to them. A man has to convince them that he is the right man. And I think you might be that right man, Abe."

Abe was astounded. "Do you want me to run for the legislature?"

"Yes, I do, Abe."

The legislature? Abe, a man of the people? Abe mumbled, "It can't hurt me too much to try."

The doctor said, "Abe, you have more than the skill to debate. You have the courage of a believer who knows he is serving God by serving men and women."

The more Abe thought about it the more eager he got. It was almost too good to be true. He hadn't lived in New Salem one year yet, and he was going to run for Illinois legislature. Maybe he would amount to something.

He thought of a plan to get elected, too.

He practiced his speech in the store, "Friends, I know a thing or two about rivers." He tucked his thumbs under imaginary suspenders. "I've been busy boating over the Sangamon River measuring depths and plotting them on maps I made. New Salem has a great future for river commerce. I want you to vote for me because I can offer you something that the other candidates can't offer you—a plan for prosperity." Abe raised his hands to the ceiling and went up on his toes.

IT WAS ALMOST TOO GOOD TO BE TRUE

ABRAHAM LINCOLN

Jack Armstrong rushed in. "Come on, Abe. A rider is here with a message from the Governor!"

"What is going on?" Abe loped out the door. He found himself out in the street with dozens of other men.

The rider shouted, "Chief Black Hawk is on the warpath! Up in northern Illinois. We need men to fight!"

Fight! War! Abe couldn't believe his ears. He had never seen an Indian who was really living in the wild like a Indian. Tom told him how his father—Abe's grandpappy Abraham—was shot dead by an Indian right in front of Tom. Uncle Mord told the same story. But it didn't seem real to Abe. Besides, Abe knew Indians had been cheated by white men. Maybe as much as black folks.

Abe argued with himself. Indians had been wronged. But could he stand by doing nothing while

"CHIEF BLACK HAWK IS ON THE WARPATH"

innocent settlers were killed? And he knew some white men who hated Indians. What if only that kind of white man volunteered to fight? Indian women and children might be murdered.

Abe volunteered.

He had to borrow a horse. He rode hard to join sixty men gathered at a village called Richland. There was a real army officer there standing behind stacks of muskets. The officer barked, "Who is your captain?"

Jack Armstrong yelled, "I intend to come back alive. I want Abe Lincoln for a captain. Abe can whip anybody."

Abe was stunned. How could he lead men into war? He was relieved when another man yelled, "I want Bill Kirkpatrick for captain!"

Men surged toward Abe and Kirkpatrick. Three times as many men surrounded Abe. "That settles

"I WANT ABE LINCOLN FOR A CAPTAIN!"

it," cried the Army officer. "Abe Lincoln here is captain of this company of mounted volunteers. Get your muskets and ride north, men."

Abe had never been so proud. He had been "elected" the leader of sixty men. He remembered the Bible. Pride was dangerous. He kept that thought in his head as the company rode north to find Black Hawk.

Abe never even saw Chief Black Hawk. But he learned about brave men who volunteered for such hardship. He learned what an officer has to do to keep order. His company seemed always one camp away from the fight. He knew that because they arrived the next day to bury the dead. The sight of the dead men haunted him.

Abe re-enlisted twice anyway. Once he saved the life of a friendly Indian who was about to be killed by some soldiers.

HE SAVED THE LIFE OF A FRIENDLY INDIAN

When the war was over, Abe felt like he had served with honor. He had been called to duty and he went. He didn't have to shoot another man. He accepted that fate as God's plan.

He returned to New Salem three weeks before the election. He found out his job as a clerk was gone. The man who owned the store was gone, too. Abe didn't have time to worry. He campaigned hard. He showed his charts of the Sangamon River and rattled off figures. He lost.

The doctor said "Don't be bitter, Abe."

Abe wasn't bitter. He figured God didn't think he was ready to be a lawmaker in the legislature. He knew the voters didn't think he was ready. Abe studied law all the harder. But he had to earn a living too. He didn't have his clerk's job.

A man offered him a chance to be his partner in a general store. Abe jumped at the chance. He used

HE CAMPAIGNED HARD

the $125 he received for his service in the Mounted Volunteers. But Abe's partner was reckless. The business borrowed more and more money. Finally no one would loan them more money. The store closed. Abe had debts to pay off. He had failed at business. He was only twenty-three and deep in debt.

He still had a good reputation. For the next two years he earned his living any way he could. He taught himself how to survey and earned money that way. He worked as the postmaster. He clerked in several stores. He wrote simple contracts for folks. He never lost his sense of humor. And he never lost the conviction that God had a plan for him.

Abe was a fearless storyteller around other men. But he drew inside his shell around women. He felt more than ever he was too uneducated, too uncultured, too awkward, and too ugly. He was twenty-five years old now. He wanted a wife, but he couldn't

HE NEVER LOST THE CONVICTION THAT GOD HAD A PLAN FOR HIM

act natural around women. He froze up. He liked Ann Rutledge enough to actually approach her and speak to her. But he learned her heart belonged to another man, even though that man had gone away from New Salem. Ann said she would never give up hope.

In two short years Abe had failed as a politician and a businessman. Would he also fail ever to win a woman's heart? Abe knew the Bible. The saints failed too—many times. Suffering made a man stronger.

So he ran for the Illinois legislature again.

He called himself a Whig this time because Henry Clay of Kentucky was a Whig. Tom Lincoln told Abe years before that Henry Clay was a man to admire: Clay was against slavery. Clay was for a strong nation. Abe liked Clay, too. Abe was more relaxed running for election this time. He failed

SUFFERING MADE A MAN STRONGER

once. And he would probably fail this time, too. So he told jokes. He had no elaborate plan for the Sangamon River.

And he won the election.

"Abe," said the doctor. "You won the election because folks knew you will do what is right."

In no time at all, Abe found himself among eight hundred people living in Vandalia, the state capitol of Illinois. Again he threw himself into a new situation, nervous about being unprepared and unworthy. He bought his first suit. But he still felt like a gawky, shaggy colt in the midst of prancing shiny thoroughbreds.

John Stuart had just been elected for the second time. John liked the modest giant from New Salem who could tell stories. He took Abe around Vandalia with him. That was wonderful for Abe, who felt so unsure of himself in "fine" company. Stuart knew

"FOLKS KNOW YOU WILL DO WHAT IS RIGHT"

exactly how to act in every social situation. Abe studied his every move and learned fast. And he learned something else. Many of the lawyers in the state capitol had taught themselves law and passed the examination to get a law license. Now Abe knew he had been right in studying law by himself. He studied law all the harder.

Within two years, Abe passed the law examination. He was a real lawyer. As if to remind Abe, life is fragile and unpredictable, Ann Rutledge got a fever and died. She never married.

Abe was re-elected. Illinois moved its state capital to Springfield. Abe roomed there with merchant Josh Speed, who soon became his close friend. Abe opened a law office with John Stuart. He got re-elected again in 1838. He was successful in every way but two. He still owed money in New Salem. And he wanted a wife—even if the Bible did assure

HE WAS A REAL LAWYER

him it was no disgrace not to have a wife. He praye
for God's will to be done.

At a party in December 1839, John Stuart intro
duced Abe to his cousin Mary Todd. She was all th
things Abe feared most in a woman. She was so tin
he gawked down at the part in her fawn brown hai
He felt like Goliath. She had a turned-up nose and
sharp chin. She was very pretty. He felt uglier tha
ever. She was perky. Her ivory skin flushed pink a
she laughed. He felt like a slow, lumbering bear. Sh
was from a very rich family in Kentucky. Could h
ever tell such a lady he grew up in a crowded on
room cabin?

She smiled "I'm a Whig, too, Mr. Lincoln."

Abe couldn't believe such a pretty lady kne
politics at all. But he would be polite. "Why is tha
Miss Todd?"

"Why, I've been a Whig ever since I met Hen
Clay."

"I'M A WHIG, TOO, MR. LINCOLN"

"Henry Clay!" He was amazed.

"Mr. Clay is a friend of my father's." Mary Todd gave Abe a look that pierced his heart like an arrow. There was no mistaking what her look meant!

A LOOK THAT PIERCED HIS HEART LIKE AN ARROW

THEY SEEMED MEANT FOR EACH OTHER

CHAPTER 7

Mary Todd actually liked him!

Abe thought he might actually like her, too. As Mary brightly talked politics, which Abe loved, she became more and more precious in his eyes. Yes, he liked her very much.

They were so unlike each other. And yet they seemed meant for each other. They saw each other often. They became engaged to be married. Marriage would have been soon if Mary's sister hadn't opposed it. Her sister's objections were so true that they hurt Abe. He was ten years older than Mary. Worst of all, he still owed money. He couldn't buy Mary the fine things she was used to having.

Abe crumbled under his doubts. He broke off the engagement. He slipped into a deep depression some folks called the "blues."

He asked God, "How could I ever be good enough for such a fine lady?"

Abe was soon to learn God's plans for us can be very complicated. Abe's friend, Josh Speed, who had moved to Kentucky, was going through the same doubts before he married his sweetheart, Fanny. Abe visited him. Abe could counsel someone else's fears with cool, calm logic.

Josh's mother knew Abe was having problems, too. She gave Abe a beautiful white Bible. "This really is the best cure for your blues, Abe."

By the time the visit was over, Josh was cured. Abe confessed to Josh, "I believe God made me an instrument of bringing Fanny and you together...."

He didn't tell Josh he was cured of the blues, too. Because he wasn't sure he could make things right with Mary. He humiliated her when he broke the engagement.

HE HUMILIATED HER WHEN HE BROKE THE ENGAGEMENT

He visited Mary to ask for forgiveness. Mary was wonderful about it. They agreed to stay friends. Mary wrote letters to a newspaper poking fun at one of Abe's political rivals. Politics in those days could erupt into more than a battle of words—Abe's friend John Stuart and Steven Douglas debated each other once with their fists.

Abe's political rival erupted, too. After he saw the letters to the newspaper, he challenged Abe to a duel. Abe could have said Mary wrote the letters. But he took the blame. He figured he couldn't talk his way out of a duel with an apology. He couldn't. It seemed like a bad dream.

Abe got to pick the place and the weapons. He sent details to his rival. They would meet in the woods along the Mississippi River near St. Louis. Each would fight with the kind of long flat sword used by soldiers in the cavalry. The two duelists had

HE CHALLENGED ABE TO A DUEL

to stay always within a rectangle 10 feet by 12 feet. Abe's friends thought his choice of weapons was a joke meant to make his rival see how foolish they were both acting.

His rival didn't think it was a joke. He showed up with two swords at the edge of the great river. Abe arrived, too. Friends for both duelists managed to talk Abe's rival out of dueling only at the last second.

If any of Abe's friends had ever seen him swing an ax they would have known he wasn't joking about using swords. Not one man in a thousand could withstand one of Abe's colossal strokes. He would have split the man like a pine log. Abe shuddered to think what might have happened. He was so ashamed that he would never talk about it again. He promised God he would grin and walk away from a fight the rest of his life—even if he didn't feel like grinning.

Mary was thrilled. She didn't know Abe was

HE WAS SO ASHAMED

ashamed. He hid it. She thought Abe was very brave to protect her. That bizarre incident brought them back together.

Abe and Mary married in November 1842. Etched inside Mary's wedding band were the words: "Love is Eternal."

The next years were busy, look-straight-ahead years of an ambitious man's life. Abe continued to build his political reputation. But he didn't run for legislature again. He had to get out of debt. He "rode the circuit" which meant he was a lawyer who rode out to take cases from folks in villages and rural areas. He was gone six months out of the year. But it was the surest, honest way Abe knew to make money fast.

The first years were very difficult for Mary. Her sister had been right. The Mary who once wore the fanciest clothes could now afford nothing fancy. The

ABE AND MARY MARRIED IN NOVEMBER 1842

Mary who once lived in a mansion now lived above a tavern. Son Bobby was born. He was a rowdy boy. When Abe came back from the circuit he would comfort Mary. Then he would have to go out and work harder.

Finally, there was light at the end of the tunnel. Abe was completely out of debt. They bought a fine, white two-story frame house in downtown Springfield. Abe was very proud of Mary. She had endured the hardship. Bobby and their next son, Eddie, had a nice fenced-in yard to play in.

Abe took young lawyer Billy Herndon into his law practice. Abe was setting the stage for a new phase of his career. He was planning to run for the U.S. House of Representatives the next year. That meant he and Mary would have to live in Washington, D.C. That meant Billy Herndon had to keep their law practice alive until Abe got back to Springfield.

THEY BOUGHT A FINE, WHITE TWO-STORY FRAME HOUSE

Mary didn't think much of Abe's new partner. Billy was cocky. He was a chatterbox who thought he could figure everybody out. He was wild, too, preferring the tavern to church. He griped about some of Abe's habits. His complaints got back to Mary. Billy didn't like the way Abe came in and read newspapers out loud every morning. Billy didn't like the way Bobby and Eddie came in and roughhoused in their law office.

Abe knew all of that about Billy, too. But he knew something else. Billy was completely loyal to him. Maybe Billy complained. But no one else could complain about Abe in front of Billy. Billy would challenge them on the spot.

Abe forgave Billy's faults. And Billy forgave Abe his faults. They loved each other like brothers. Abe knew he would be leaving his law practice in faithful hands if he won the election.

ABE FORGAVE BILLY'S FAULTS

He won the election. Abe and his family left for Washington, D.C., in January 1848. About half of the 227 members of the House of Representatives belonged to the Democrat political party. The other half belonged to the Whig party. The President was Democrat James Polk. Polk had waged war against Mexico for two years. Some Whigs like Abe thought this was really a war to get more land and extend slavery—because the Missouri Compromise arranged by Henry Clay allowed new states to the south to have slavery. Of course, at the time of the compromise, Henry Clay didn't think there would ever be any new states to the south. The war with Mexico would change all that.

Abe took a strong stand against the war. He expected the other Whigs to back him up. But they didn't.

One Whig told him, "Why make the slavery people

ABE TOOK A STRONG STAND AGAINST THE WAR

mad? Let's just hope nothing bad happens."

Abe had spoken out against slavery before. Now he was going to do something about it. He was going to introduce a bill that would phase out slavery in Washington, D.C., if Congress would vote in favor of his bill. He figured that would be a small start toward solving a monstrous problem.

Another Whig found out his plan. He asked Abe, "Have you lost your senses? Don't you know that bill will make the slavery people furious?"

Abe was disappointed in his fellow Whigs once again. But he campaigned hard for Zachary Taylor, the Whig candidate for President in the 1848 election. Abe was meeting other powerful people in the Whig party, too. They found out how capable he was. But after Taylor won the election, Abe found out what they really thought of him. After every Presidential election, the new President appointed hundreds of people to judgeships, commissions, and

"THAT BILL WILL MAKE THE SLAVERY PEOPLE FURIOUS"

other government agencies. Abe gave the new president, Taylor, a modest list of qualified people from Illinois. Not one person on his list was appointed.

Abe soon found out President Taylor and other Whig leaders thought he was too pushy. He was too outspoken. Why irritate the Democrats and slave-owners? There could be a war between the free states and slave states. No one wanted war.

The leading Whigs had lots of experience. Abe thought it over long and hard. His final conclusion made his blood run cold: Unless reasonable people solved the slavery problem soon there would be a war anyway. The entire United States, such a promising young nation founded on such wonderful ideals of freedom, might go up in flames. He was overwhelmed with sadness.

What was Abe supposed to do? The others in his own Whig political party refused to listen to him. He

THE ENTIRE UNITED STATES ... MIGHT GO UP IN FLAMES

prayed for God's help.

After that, for some reason he could think of nothing but Mary. Her father had recently died. She had gone home to Kentucky for a while. She had to force herself to return. She didn't like Washington, D.C. She thought the people were snobs. In spite of her own rich family, Mary had never been a snob. What other rich young lady would have openly embraced a rough country lawyer like Abe Lincoln?

Abe's heart ached. Mary had endured hardship for him and the boys. Just when they moved into a nice home in Springfield and Mary was her bubbly self again, Abe yanked her away from it. Now his sweet little Mary was unhappy again. God must be telling him to fix that.

One evening after they put the boys to bed, Abe said, "Mary, we need to make a powerful big decision."

"MARY, WE NEED TO MAKE A POWERFUL BIG DECISION"

EDDIE, NOT YET FOUR YEARS OLD, DIED

CHAPTER 8

Abe put his huge paw over Mary's tiny hand. "I'm thinking of getting out of politics."

"Are you sure you want to do that?" Her voice betrayed how happy she was to hear that news.

"Why don't we go back to Springfield after my term is over?"

Mary perked up. "Maybe little Eddie would get better. He's been so sick here in Washington, D.C."

And they did return to Springfield. Abe plunged into his law practice with his loyal partner Billy Herndon. Mary loved her big house. But their joy was short-lived. Eddie, not yet four years old, died. Mary sunk into the depths of despair. She was touched to see a poem in the local newspaper entitled "Little Eddie":

And the angel of death was hovering up high
And the lovely boy was called to die
Bright is the home to him now given
For such is the kingdom of heaven.

The newspaper didn't reveal who wrote the poem. But Mary knew who wrote it. Abe wrote it. He was sure Eddie was in heaven. He had to make sure Mary knew it too.

Mary began to feel better. When Mary found out she was going to have another baby, both she and Abe were sure the baby was God's gift.

Willie was born in December 1850.

About the same time Abe found out that his father Tom was deathly sick. Abe had drifted apart from his father. He couldn't resolve whatever difference he had with his father and he wouldn't talk about it. That's the way Abe was with a problem he couldn't

ABE FOUND OUT THAT HIS FATHER WAS DEATHLY SICK

solve. He didn't complain. He didn't gossip. He did what the Bible said, he prayed and he hoped.

He wrote his stepbrother John and urged him to tell his father Tom to trust "our great, and good, and merciful maker" and "if it is to be his lot to go now, he will soon have a joyous meeting with many loved ones gone before...."

One month later Abe's father, Tom, died.

Death seemed to pull Abe closer to God. More and more of his loved ones were in God's Paradise. Abe accepted God's dominion with all his heart and mind.

He told a preacher at the time, "I examine the issues of life and death as rigorously as I examine any issue in a courtroom. I always conclude that divine authority and inspiration of the Bible are absolute certainties."

The next years were golden. In 1853, baby Tom

ABE ACCEPTED GOD'S DOMINION WITH ALL HIS HEART

was born. He wiggled like a little tadpole. Abe always called him Tad. Bobby was now almost ten and Willie was three. The house was noisy. The boys were healthy. Mary was happy.

Abe practiced law, which he loved. His image as a skilled lawyer with a great sense of humor was set in these happy, relaxed years. Abe had thousands of stories he could tell to make a point. Some were funny and some were not. He didn't make up stories. He collected them. He was a masterful storyteller who never seemed to forget even one line of a story after he heard it.

He had the Bible memorized, too. It was due to his habit of always reading aloud. He felt by using the two senses of hearing and seeing instead of just one sense of seeing he could remember almost anything he read. He could quote by heart all the Psalms, entire chapters of Isaiah, and almost all of the New

THE BOYS WERE HEALTHY... MARY WAS HAPPY

Testament. He used verses from the Bible to make points, too. And his favorite method of persuasion he learned from the Bible. Abe knew Jesus told parables because most folks remembered entertaining stories much longer than they remembered preaching.

Abe might have spent the rest of his life practicing law in Springfield if he hadn't read one morning in his newspaper about Stephen Douglas running for re-election to the U.S. Senate in 1858.

"Billy!" Abe turned a stunned face to his law partner. "It says here Douglas wants every state to vote whether it wants slavery! Even the sates where black people are now free!" Abe groaned. "The problem of slavery just won't go away. It's going to get worse!"

Billy sighed. "You're the only man in Illinois who can beat Stephen Douglas."

"THE PROBLEM OF SLAVERY JUST WON'T GO AWAY!"

"I don't want to go back to Washington, D.C...."
Abe paused. "But what choice do I have now?"

The race for the position of Illinois Senator
wouldn't have attracted much attention in earlier
years. But Douglas had become a national figure.
He had personally destroyed the "Missouri Compromise" in 1854 when he devilishly pushed through a
change in the law that allowed any state to adopt
slavery. He was the man who spoke for slavery. He
was a powerful speaker, too, so gifted he could make
decent folks think slavery was all right. There was
only one way to prevent that.

Abe said to Billy, "I'll debate him."

"That rascal is too smart to debate you."

The old Whig party had disintegrated over slavery.
A new political party called the Republican party
formed against slavery. At their convention, Abe
gave a speech that used the Savior's own words, "A

DOUGLAS HAD BECOME A NATIONAL FIGURE

house divided against itself cannot stand." Abe added, "I believe this government cannot endure, permanently half slave and half free."

His speech was published in newspapers all over Illinois and even in New York. Some editors were so impressed they published the entire speech as a small book.

When Douglas heard this new Republican party nominated Abe Lincoln as their candidate for the Senate seat from Illinois he muttered, "I'll have my hands full now. Abe is the best stump speaker in the west."

Only Mary Todd Lincoln was unhappier than Douglas. But Mary knew politics. She knew this race was much bigger that just a Senate race. It was slavery against freedom. It might make Abe a national figure.

Abe showed up at the first rally for Douglas.

IT WAS SLAVERY AGAINST FREEDOM

Douglas was amused. He even invited Abe up on the platform. Abe spoke to the same crowd the next day. Abe destroyed everything Douglas had said.

At the next rally for Douglas, Abe was there again. The next day he gave his speech, ripping apart Douglas's speech. Douglas was no longer amused.

Abe kept following Douglas around Illinois, blasting apart his opponent's speeches. Newspaper reporters soon realized that both he and Douglas were magnificent speakers. The New York newspapers said, "Illinois is the most interesting political battleground in the United States."

Douglas finally realized Abe had outsmarted him. By always speaking last, Abe was hammering the last nail in every time. What could he do about it?

Abe offered a suggestion, "Debate me on the same day."

And Douglas was trapped.

DOUGLAS WAS NO LONGER AMUSED

They agreed to travel around the state to have a total of seven debates. Mary was thrilled now. She wished Abe good luck and blurted, "Now I know you'll be President someday, Abe."

"President!" Abe was amazed. He could only laugh.

Abe prayed for God's help. He would speak the truth during the debates, whether that was politically smart or not. He would urge folks to honor the Declaration of Independence: All men are created equal.

Douglas created fear. Did folks want blacks flooding into Illinois? Did they want blacks marrying their daughters? Did they want blacks riding in the same carriages? Eating in the same inns? In spite of Douglas's treachery, Abe got 190,000 votes and Douglas got 176,000 votes. But the Senator wasn't elected by popular vote. The newly-elected Illinois

"PRESIDENT!" HE COULD ONLY LAUGH

state representatives voted for the Senator. And Democrats outnumbered Republicans fifty-four to forty-six.

Abe lost the election!

But both men now were national figures. Both were seen—even in the east—as the best spokesmen their political parties had to offer. Two years later these two men got the nominations from their parties to run for President. But to show how divided the country was over slavery, two more political parties formed. Four men would be on the ballot for President.

It was the same debate all over again. Abe campaigned hard for President and made his position as plain and honest as he could. He was like Henry Clay. He hated slavery and would not allow any states to leave the Union!

On election day, Abe hung around the telegraph office in Springfield to hear some early results. He

ABE HUNG AROUND THE TELEGRAPH OFFICE

was winning the popular vote for President. But he had won the popular vote before. Would he lose once again because the rules were strange? Each state was allotted a certain number of "electoral votes," according to how many people lived in that state. But the winner of the popular vote in that state got all the electoral votes whether he won the popular vote by one vote or 100,000 votes! So, even in the national election, it was possible to win the popular vote and lose the election anyway.

Abe walked back to wait with Mary at their home. In 1860 it took a very long time to total up all the votes around the nation.

Abe thanked God for his chance. How many men got to run for President? Now he would just have to wait and see God's plan.

Would God decide Abe should fail again?

Mary said, "You should grow a beard, Abe."

WOULD GOD DECIDE ABE SHOULD FAIL AGAIN ?

"Why? I've never had a beard my whole life. I'r fifty-one years old, Mary."

She smiled. "A beard will make the new Presider look so dignified."

Abe laughed. "I will grow a beard. God knows need all the help I can get." Abe could always laug at himself. When some folks called him a gorill Abe just laughed and said, "I'm a bit smarter I hope

There was a knock on the door. The minute the saw Billy Herndon's face Abe and Mary knew th answer....

ABE AND MARY KNEW THE ANSWER...

"HOWDY DO, MR. PRESIDENT!"

CHAPTER 9

A smile almost split Billy's face into two halves. He yelled, "Howdy do, Mr. President!"

Giant Abe and tiny Mary danced a jig. The three boys hooped and hollered. Mary was even cordial to Billy Herndon. Abe fell into deep silence. The days ahead would be very dangerous. The slave states knew Abe was going to be very tough on slavery. They might strike quickly.

In early 1861, Abe stood on the platform at the back of a passenger train, saying farewell to his good friends of Springfield. His words were very sad. "I now leave, not knowing when or whether ever I may return, with a task before me greater than that which rested upon George Washington. Without the assistance of that Divine Being who ever attended him, I cannot succeed. With that assistance, I cannot fail."

That summed it up completely. God would decide.

All over the nation, men were drifting apart, silently taking sides. The slave states attracted many good men—men Abe knew. These men chose to defend their land and their families. Abe was very saddened by that. In making that choice, they were defending a terrible evil.

Abe was sworn in as President on March 4, 1861. He hardly had time to help Mary and the three boys get settled in the White House, the mansion for the President and his family in Washington, D.C. The slave states struck quickly. Calling themselves the Confederacy, their army attacked the United States army at Fort Sumter in South Carolina on April 12 The war had begun!

Two days later Fort Sumter surrendered to the Confederates. Abe's heart ached when he got the

THE WAR HAD BEGUN!

reports of how many men had been killed. He mourned the men on both sides. This was a terrible national problem that men like himself had failed to solve. Now young men were solving the problem with their blood.

The tone of the war soon became obvious. Abe's United States Army, now called the Union Army, had vastly superior resources and numbers of men. The Confederacy had vastly superior officers. The main Union generals were timid. Abe felt like King Saul. South of Washington, D.C., there was Goliath in the person of brilliant General Robert E. Lee, standing out in the open every day, laughing and taunting the Union Army. Where was Abe's David?

In July, Abe proclaimed a national day for fasting and repenting sins. He said, "It is fit and becoming in all people, at all times, to acknowledge and revere the Supreme Government of God...to confess and

GOLIATH IN THE PERSON OF GENERAL ROBERT E. LEE

deplore their sins and transgressions in the full conviction that the fear of the Lord is the beginning of wisdom."

Cynical politicians were stunned. Who was this new president in the White House?

Abe waited and waited for a Union victory. People of the Union became upset with him. Why couldn't the Union Army fight? One of Abe's own advisors grumbled sarcastically, "Our Union Army is dug in and watching the enemy as fast as it can."

Influential people began to tell Abe to give up and let the Confederacy go its own way. The Confederacy was perfectly willing to have a standoff. Lee and his generals were brilliant at defense. If the Confederates held out long enough, all the people in the Union might finally say "Stop. That's enough."

Abe was heard to say, "I am a humble instrument in the hands of our heavenly Father. He permits the

INFLUENTIAL PEOPLE BEGAN TO TELL ABE TO GIVE UP

war to go on for some wise purpose of His own, mysterious and unknown to us...." Again, the cynics shook their heads.

Suddenly, son Willie died. Mary became bedridden because she was grieving so hard. Abe prayed hard. He felt like only his faith kept him from losing his mind. How much suffering could he and Mary bear?

Word drifted in of some small Union victories along the Mississippi River. A general named Ulysses Grant seemed to be responsible.

"What kind of general is this Ulysses Grant?" asked Abe.

His advisors shrugged. "He wasn't even in the Army when the war started. He has the reputation of being unreliable."

That was a polite way of saying Grant drank too much alcohol. Abe thought about it. He despised the

"WHAT KIND OF GENERAL IS THIS ULYSSES GRANT?"

effects of too much alcohol. But he considered alcoholics sick people, not evil people. Besides people can change. Maybe Grant didn't have a drinking problem anymore. He would wait to see if this "unreliable" General Grant had any more success.

Grant did have more success. His Union Army was moving down the Mississippi, winning battle after battle. Grant was cutting the Confederacy in two!

Abe thanked God. He issued a proclamation of thanksgiving: "It is right to recognize and confess the presence of the Almighty Father...invoke the influence of His Holy Spirit to subdue the anger, which has produced and so long sustained a needless and cruel rebellion...."

Wise people in the Union began to understand Abe. God was the master of history. Abe was his

GRANT WAS CUTTING THE CONFEDERACY IN TWO!

instrument. Never had an American politician stated it so plainly.

There were really two wars now. The war in the west was being won by the Union Army under Grant's relentless offensive tactics. The war in the east was being won by the Confederacy under Lee's clever defensive tactics.

Suddenly General Lee was no longer on the defensive. He moved his Confederate Army north into the Union state of Pennsylvania. Abe tried to think like Lee. What was he doing? Lee must think the Confederacy was in trouble. Grant was capturing the west. If Lee could now lead the Confederates north right smack into the Union and win a big battle in the east, the Union might lose heart. Abe had to admit Lee was brilliant.

In a meeting with his closest advisors Abe said, "We are not doing enough. God will help our Union

"GOD WILL HELP OUR UNION ARMY..."

Army drive Lee out of Pennsylvania and we will free all the slaves in the United States, including the Confederacy." His advisors were stunned. Some said that was a terrible mistake.

But Abe prepared his Emancipation Proclamation. On September 22, 1862, he proclaimed that on the next New Year's Day the slaves of the southern states were to be set free. And on January 1, 1863, he declared all slaves free!

In July, Lee struck at Gettysburg in Pennsylvania. It was a bloody battle. Commanders used tactics from the old musket days. But their soldiers were armed with modern rifles. The slaughter was horrible. The Union prevailed. Lee retreated back to the slave states. Almost the same day, Grant won another great battle. He captured Vicksburg, a fortress along the Mississippi River long considered impossible to conquer. The Union controlled the west!

HE DECLARED ALL SLAVES FREE !

ABRAHAM LINCOLN

In November, Abe appeared at the Gettysburg battlefield with a speech of a mere 268 words. He began, "Four score and seven years ago our fathers brought forth on this continent, a new nation conceived in liberty..." And he concluded with, "We here highly resolve that these dead shall not have died in vain; that this nation, under God, shall have a new birth of freedom; and that government of the people, by the people, for the people, shall not perish from the earth."

Abe knew the Bible by heart. He knew sinful nations did perish. Some newspapers thought his speech was trivial because it was so short. But several recognized it as a masterpiece.

Back in Washington, D.C., Abe got a mild disease similar to chicken pox. He joked, "At last, I have something I can give everyone."

Abe rarely lost his sense of humor, even through

"FOUR SCORE AND SEVEN YEARS AGO..."

those terrible days. Humor helped him cope with the constant heartbreak of war. More than one person observed Abe was the saddest looking man they had ever seen—until they heard him joke. Then a smile transformed his face into radiant joy.

But in the beginning of 1864, the war in the east was once again bogged down. Abe simply had no general in the east who could fight. He prayed. The answer was obvious. Like Saul, Abe had his David. Abe must let him fight.

He said to his advisors, "I don't care what people say about Grant. The man fights."

He put Grant in charge of the entire Union Army: the most awesome military force ever assembled by mankind, over two hundred thousand men armed to the teeth with modern rifles and heavy artillery pieces.

The outcome seemed inevitable. But Abe was not

"I DON'T CARE WHAT PEOPLE SAY ABOUT GRANT"

jubilant. He knew what this meant. The two great generals of the war now opposed each other in the east. Losses on both sides would be staggering. It was heartbreaking to think about how terrible it would be.

And suddenly the outcome was not inevitable at all. Abe had to get re-elected president in 1864.

The two armies were deadlocked, slaughtering each other. The people of the Union were sick of the war and the bloodbath. The man running against Abe was none other than McClellan, one of the Union generals in the east Abe had fired—a very weak indecisive man who couldn't fight!

McClellan confirmed it. He said if he was president, he would stop the war right away—the Confederacy could come back in the Union and keep their slaves!

Abe found out men in his own Republican Party

THE MAN RUNNING AGAINST ABE WAS McCLELLAN

were plotting to find a Republican candidate other than Abe. They didn't think Abe had a chance of being re-elected.

Never in his worst dreams did Abe think the whole struggle might end up resolving nothing. He went down on his knees. Surely God would not let this happen now.

SURELY GOD WOULD NOT LET THIS HAPPEN NOW

"I HAVE NO TIME FOR QUARRELS"

CHAPTER 10

Abe's great struggle to free the slaves seemed doomed. Abe knew God was never wrong. What was happening?

He had prayed so many times, "Oh please, God, give me the wisdom to know what you want me to do." Had Abe made a mistake? Had he not understood God's wishes?

He just had to continue to do what he thought was right. He began to plan how he might persuade the new President McClellan to carry through with the struggle.

Mary asked, "How can you even talk to that weakling? He failed you time and time again."

"I have no time for quarrels. There's too much to do."

But in his heart Abe knew Mary was right. McClellan would fail. He had failed Abe before—

again and again.

If only Grant could defeat Lee soon. But it wasn't likely. Lee seemed determined to fight to the last man. After all, Lee knew McClellan was the answer to the Confederacy's prayers.

Abe prayed too. It was September 1864.

Eleven-year-old Tad burst into Abe's office. "General Sherman has taken Atlanta!"

Far away from the Grant-Lee struggle in the east, the Union general Sherman had captured the great rail center of the Confederacy in the south. It was an awful blow to the Confederacy.

There was hope for the Union yet. Now if only Grant's army could finish off Lee's army. But Lee's army fought on doggedly. Lee knew exactly what was at stake: If Lincoln was not re-elected, McClellan would let the slave states keep their slaves—the Confederacy would win after all!

The presidential election in early November crept

"GENERAL SHERMAN HAS TAKEN ATLANTA!"

closer and closer. It was now the middle of October.

Abe stared at his office door. *If only dear little Tad would fling that door open again and hop in with good news. Oh, please, God....*

The door flung open!

Tad yelled, "General Sheridan has routed Jubal Early. We've captured the Shenandoah Valley!"

Once again the Union had scored a giant success away from the long bloody battle between Grant and Lee. The Shenandoah Valley in Virginia was vital to the Confederacy. Its fertile soil was a major source of their food.

"Thank God," said Abe. It was all Abe needed to say.

The people of the Union now saw an end to the struggle. They had believed in Abe back in 1860. They sometimes lost faith in Abe. But now in 1864 they believed in him again.

The election results trickled in.

"THANK GOD"

ABRAHAM LINCOLN

Abe remembered the election four years earlier. So much had happened since then. He truly felt he had become an instrument of God. And he was at peace while he waited. He had done what he thought God wanted. He hadn't been lazy about it as if God would just give him the answers. He had devoted his entire heart and soul to winning the war.

Abe won 55 percent of the popular vote and won almost all the electoral votes. Once again, Abe was elected President of the United States.

The struggle to free the slaves and preserve the Union was as good as done. The presidency remained in Abe's giant hands. And Abe was in God's cosmic hands.

Abe was very tired. The fatigue seemed to settle in now and weigh him down. Abe almost seemed to shrink. If he had been a young man, he would have bounced up and looked toward his next struggle. But he knew this struggle was his last one.

NCE AGAIN, ABE WAS PRESIDENT OF THE UNITED STATES

Abe was sworn in as president a second time. In a speech full of quotes from the Bible he said, "The judgments of the Lord are true and righteous altogether. With malice toward none; with charity for all; with firmness in the right, as God gives us to see the right, let us strive on to finish the work we are in...."

In early April of 1865 Abe had a dream. He told Mary and some close friends about it. He dreamed he heard sobbing. He began wandering through the White House. He saw soldiers guarding a coffin. Abe asked a soldier "Who is the dead man in that coffin?" The soldier answered "Sir, it's the president. He was murdered by a crazy man."

"Oh no!" gasped Mary.

Mary and their close friends were very sad. Abe seemed genuinely in touch with God. They knew men in the Bible got dreams from angels. Could Abe's dream become true?

ABE HAD A DREAM

But the dream was forgotten. Because on April 9, 1845, Abe got a telegram. Lee had surrendered to Grant. The war was over.

People celebrated wildly throughout the Union. Even people in the Confederacy were glad the war was over. They had suffered tremendously. And now they were thankful the terms of peace would be in the hands of a kind giant like Abe.

It was time to relax. On April 14 Abe took Mary to the Ford Theater in Washington, D.C., to watch a play. One of the actors was a twenty-seven-year-old weak man, too cowardly to have fought in the great struggle. He was crazy too. He wanted to take revenge for the Confederacy. He was too crazy to know what he wanted to do would cause his own Confederacy untold suffering.

The man sneaked up behind Abe and shot him in the head. Furious Union soldiers finally trapped the murderer days later, hiding in a barn like a rat, and

THE WORLD MOURNED HIS LOSS

shot him to death. Abe would not have approved of the soldiers shooting his murderer without a trial. But Abe was dead.

Abe Lincoln died the morning of April 15, 1865.

The Union mourned the loss of their great leader. Wise people in the Confederacy mourned his loss, too. When General Sherman told a Confederate general that Abe was dead, the blood drained from the Confederate general's face. He said, "The Confederacy lost the best friend we had."

The world mourned his loss, too. The great Russian writer Tolstoy said Abe's moral power and strength of character made him the greatest figure in world history since Bible times.